Madonna
in My Pocket

Madonna
in My Pocket

Christina Rodenbeck

RYLAND
PETERS
& SMALL
LONDON NEW YORK

Designer Saskia Janssen
Editor Miriam Hyslop
Picture Researcher Emily Westlake
Production Controller Deborah Wehner
Art Director Gabriella Le Grazie
Publishing Director Alison Starling

First published in the
United States in 2004
by Ryland Peters & Small, Inc.
519 Broadway
5th Floor
New York NY 10012
www.rylandpeters.com

10 9 8 7 6 5 4 3 2

ISBN 1 84172 729 6

Printed in China

Contents

Introduction

THE **MADONNA** IS ONE OF THE MOST **POWERFUL**
ICONS IN WORLD CULTURE. AS **VIRGIN**,
AS **HOLY MOTHER**, AND AS **SORROWING MOTHER**,
SHE HAS DOMINATED THE WESTERN **IMAGINATION**
FOR CENTURIES.

Let Mary never be far from your lips and
from your heart. Following her, you will
never sink into despair. Contemplating her,
you will never go wrong.

ST. BERNARDINO OF SIENA (14TH CENTURY)

Mary in the Bible

Mary is not a major presence in the story of Jesus as told in the Gospels. She appears only a few times and her role in Jesus' story is minimal. Yet over the centuries, her cult grew and flourished across Europe and the New World as a grassroots movement. Clearly, the worship of the Virgin fulfills a particular need for many people as expressed in the words of Paul McCartney in the Beatles song *Let It Be*: "When I find myself in times of trouble, Mother Mary comes to me speaking words of wisdom..."

Deeper Roots

Some historians argue that the Madonna we know is a continuation of ancient currents of belief. In its early years, Christianity had to compete with various other religions across the Roman Empire. One of these was the worship of Isis, the Egyptian goddess. Isis was typically depicted as a mother with a baby on her knee. Was the worship of Isis subsumed into Christianity? Pagan beliefs also tally with the Virgin's three main personae—Virgin, Mother and Mater Dolorosa (Mother of Sorrows). The ancient peoples of Europe worshipped the Triple Goddess—Virgin, Mother, and Crone, as symbolized by the monthly cycle of the Moon from New to Full to Dark. Mary has always been strongly associated with the night sky.

Mary Today

Psychologists, Jungians in particular, might argue that the cult of the Virgin Mary fills a fundamental gap in Christian theology—call it the feminine mystery—and fulfills a powerful human need for female as well as male spirituality. Perhaps it's no surprise then, that she has appeared more frequently in apparitions than any other saint or deity, and today, in Europe and the Americas, Marianism is still the most widespread, and possibly the most profoundly felt, of all cults.

Virgin & Mother

as the VIRGIN MOTHER, the MADONNA
REPRESENTS **PURITY** AND **INNOCENCE**;
SPRINGTIME AND fertility; MOTHERHOOD,
compassion, and tenderness.

...Mother of divine grace,...
Virgin most merciful,
Virgin most faithful,
Mirror of justice,
Seat of wisdom,
Cause of our joy,
Spiritual vessel,
Vessel of honor,
Singular vessel of devotion,
Mystical rose,

Tower of David,
Tower of ivory,
House of gold,
Ark of the covenant,
Gate of heaven,
Morning star,
Health of the sick,
Refuge of sinners,
Comforter of the afflicted....

THE LITANY OF LORETO

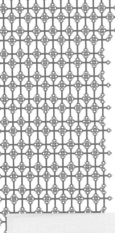

THE "HAIL MARY" IS AN ANCIENT PRAYER USED BY EARLY CHRISTIANS LONG BEFORE IT WAS AUTHORIZED BY THE CHURCH. IT IS BASED ON THE WORDS THE ANGEL GABRIEL WAS SAID TO HAVE USED IN THE ANNUNCIATION.

Ave Maria

Hail Mary, full of grace,
our Lord is with thee,
blessed art thou among women,
and blessed is the fruit of thy womb, Jesus.
Holy Mary, Mother of God,
pray for us sinners, now, and in the
hour of our death.

15

Mary and Gabriel

...Under her breasts she had
Such multitudinous burnings, to and fro,
And throbs not understood; she did not know
If they were hurt or joy for her; but only
That she was grown strange to herself, half lonely,
All wonderful, filled full of pains to come
And thoughts she dare not think, swift thoughts
   and dumb,
Human, and quaint, her own, yet very far,
Divine, dear, terrible, familiar...
Her heart was faint for telling; to relate
Her limbs' sweet treachery, her strange high estate,
Over and over, whispering, half revealing,
Weeping; and so find kindness to her healing...

RUPERT BROOKE (1887–1915)

Oh Mary,

Gentle Mother,

open the door and let me in.

A bee has stung your belly with faith.

Let me float in it like a fish.

"JESUS, THE ACTOR, PLAYS THE HOLY
GHOST," ANNE SEXTON (1928–1974)

THIS IS MARY'S RESPONSE TO THE NEWS THAT SHE
IS TO BE THE MOTHER OF GOD.

The Magnificat

My soul magnifies the Lord,
And my spirit has rejoiced in God my Saviour.
For he has regarded the lowliness of his handmaiden,
And, behold, from henceforth all generations shall
call me blessed.
For he that is mighty has done to me great things...

ST. LUKE I: 46, THE BIBLE

The May Magnificat

May is Mary's month, and I
Muse at that and wonder why:
  Her feasts follow reason,
  Dated due to season—

Candlemas, Lady Day
But the Lady Month, May,
  Why fasten that upon her,
  With a feasting in her honor?...

...

Ask of her, the mighty mother:
Her reply puts this other
  Question: What is Spring?—
  Growth in every thing—

Flesh and fleece, fur and feather,
Grass and greenworld all together;
  Star-eyed strawberry-breasted
  Throstle above her nested

Cluster of bugle blue eggs thin
Forms and warms the life within;
  And bird and blossom swell
  In sod or sheath or shell.

All things rising, all things sizing
Mary sees, sympathizing
  With that world of good,
  Nature's motherhood

...

Well but there was more than this:
Spring's universal bliss
  Much, had much to say
  To offering Mary May...

...

This ecstasy all through mothering earth
Tells Mary her mirth till Christ's birth
  To remember and exultation
  In God who was her salvation.

GERARD MANLEY HOPKINS (1844–1889)

25

Mer, mere, mère, mater, Maia, Mary,
Star of the Sea,
Mother.

"TRIBUTE TO THE ANGELS,"
HILDA DOOLITTLE (1886–1961)

The Virgin's Flowers

Bryony
Canterbury Bell
Dropwort
Flowering almond
Iris
Lady's Balsam
Lady's Seal
Ladyslippers
Lily

Lungwort
Marigold
Roses
White irises
White narcissi
Costmary
Periwinkle
Snowdrop
Violet

She is the flower, the violet,
the blossoming rose
that gives out such a scent to
satisfy us all...

GAUTIER DE COINCY (1177–1236)

Dolorosa

as the **grieving mother** of Jesus,
Mary **shares** our human **suffering**
and weeps **tears** for the world.

...Sighing Dove,
Mother of Dolors,
Fount of tears,
Sea of bitterness,
Field of tribulation,
Mass of suffering,
Mirror of patience,
Rock of constancy,
Remedy in perplexity,
Joy of the afflicted,
Ark of the desolate,
Refuge of the abandoned,
Shield of the oppressed,
Conqueror of the incredulous,
Solace of the wretched,

Medicine of the sick,

Help of the faint,

Strength of the weak,

Protectress of those who fight,

Haven of the shipwrecked,

Calmer of tempests,

Companion of the sorrowful,

...

Comfort of Widows,

Joy of all Saints,

Queen of thy Servants,

Holy Mary, who alone art unexampled,

Pray for us, most Sorrowful Virgin...

THE LITANY OF
OUR LADY OF SEVEN SORROWS

Mother of God! as evening falls
   Upon the silent sea,
And shadows veil the mountain walls,
   We lift our souls to thee!

"HYMN OF THE KNIGHTS TEMPLARS,"
JOHN HAY (1838–1905)

The Seven Sorrows of Our Lady

The Prophecy of Simeon

The Flight into Egypt

The Loss of Jesus in the Temple

Mary meets Jesus Carrying the Cross

The Crucifixion

Mary Receives the Dead Body of Her Son

The Burial of Her Son and Closing of the Tomb

The Memorare

*Remember, O most gracious Virgin Mary,
that never was it known that anyone who
fled to your protection, implored your
help or sought your intercession was left
unaided. Inspired by this confidence, I fly
unto you, O Virgin of virgins, my Mother.
To you do I come; before you I stand, sinful
and sorrowful. O mother of the Word
Incarnate, despise not my petitions, but
in your mercy, hear and answer me.*

ST. BERNARD (1090–1153)

Mamma, why have you come?

...your weeping pierces me like the sharpest sword...

CHRIST ON THE CROSS "THE PASSION"
JACOPONE DA TODI (C.1230–1306)

O Mary, come quickly to our aid.

Do not let us stray from the Fold,

The wolf is waiting to destroy us...

ST. LOMMAN (7TH CENTURY)

Queen

finally, mary ascends to heaven
where she becomes our intercessor
with god, listening to human prayers
and pleading with jesus in judgement
on our behalf.

Salve Regina

Hail, Holy Queen,
Mother of Mercy,
our life, our sweetness and our hope!
To thee do we cry, poor banished children of Eve;
to thee do we send up our sighs, mourning and
weeping in this valley of tears.
Turn then, most gracious advocate,
thine eyes of mercy toward us,
and after this our exile,
show unto us the blessed fruit of thy womb, Jesus.
O clement, O loving, O sweet Virgin Mary!

IITH CENTURY HYMN

Queen of angels,

Queen of patriarchs,

Queen of prophets,

Queen of apostles,

Queen of martyrs,

Queen of confessors,

Queen of virgins,

Queen of all saints,

Queen conceived without original sin,

Queen assumed into heaven,

Queen of the most holy Rosary,

Queen of families

Queen of peace...

THE LITANY OF LORETO

If the winds of temptation arise, if you are driven upon the rocks of tribulation, look to the star, invoke Mary. If you are tossed upon the waves of pride, of ambition, or envy, or rivalry, look to the star, invoke Mary.

ST. BERNARD

47

Mary's Emblems

Fleur-de-lis

Crescent moon

Full moon

Bees

Sacred heart

Fountain

Temple

Olive

Cypress

Girdle

Crown and scepter

Twelve stars

Mirror

Morning star

Pole star

Spearmint

Sorrel

Strawberry

Maidenhair fern

Blue mantle

Hail thou star of the sea
Portal of the sky
Ever Virgin Mother
Of the Lord Most High...
Break all captives' fetters
Light on blindness pour
Chase all evil from us
Every bliss implore...

8TH CENTURY HYMN

...O bread of life which swellst up without leaven!
O bridge which join'st together earth and heaven!
Whose eyes see me through these walls and through glass,
And through this flesh like as through cypress pass,
Behold a little heart made great by Thee,
Swelling yet shrinking in Thy majesty.
O dwell in it! For whereso'er thou go'st,
There is the temple of the Holy Ghost.

"A POEM FOR MAY" JOHN DONNE (1572–1631)

51

Symbols of Mary

The Burning Bush
The Tabernacle
The Ark of Covenant
The Manna Pot
Jacob's Ladder
Aaron's Censer
The Golden Lamp Stand
Aaron's Rod
The City of God
Ezekiel's Gate
Mount Sinai

*Mary is an arsenal of grace
and she comes to the aid of her
clients. She sustains, strengthens
and revives us by the heavenly
favors that she heaps upon us.*

ST. PAULINUS (353–431)

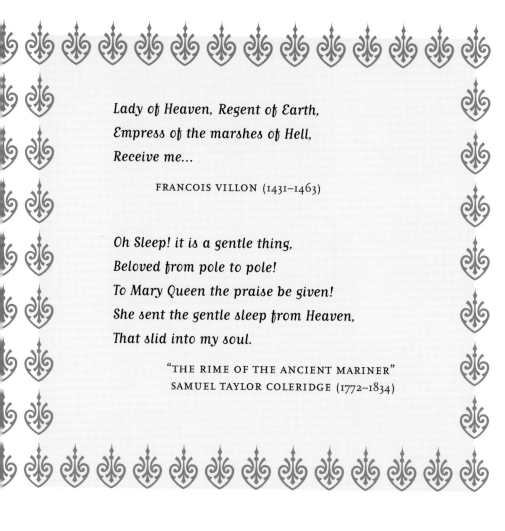

Lady of Heaven, Regent of Earth,
Empress of the marshes of Hell,
Receive me...

FRANCOIS VILLON (1431–1463)

Oh Sleep! it is a gentle thing,
Beloved from pole to pole!
To Mary Queen the praise be given!
She sent the gentle sleep from Heaven,
That slid into my soul.

"THE RIME OF THE ANCIENT MARINER"
SAMUEL TAYLOR COLERIDGE (1772–1834)

Mary in Our Midst

pilgrimages, apparitions,
and feast days.

The beauty that I saw in Our
Lady was wonderful, though
I could make out no particular
detail, only the general shape
of her face and the whiteness
and amazing splendor of her
robes, which was not dazzling
but quite soft...

ST. TERESA OF AVILA (1515–1582)

The cult of the Virgin Mary is alive and flourishing. Probably somewhere near you there is a shrine; it may even be the site of an apparition, because Mary is wont to visit people here on terra firma. Since the early days of Christianity, visitations by the Virgin have been regularly reported and in our times, Mary seems to be spotted somewhere on Earth at least once a year. Some of these visions have to be taken with a pinch of salt—or possibly stardust— but some reports have the ring of authenticity. Most of the Marian pilgrimages are to sites where an apparition or a miracle has occurred.

Most Popular Marian Pilgrimages

Lourdes, France
The young peasant girl, Bernadette Soubirous, had a vision of the Virgin at this site in 1858. Since then it has become the biggest Christian pilgrimage center in the world, after Rome and Jerusalem.

Czestochowa, Poland
The Black Madonna, alleged to be a portrait painted by St. Luke himself, attracts thousands of visitors a year. On May 3 every year there are huge celebrations in honor of Mary as Queen of Poland.

Fatima, Portugal
On May 13, 1917, the Virgin appeared to three children and told them to pray for peace. She later confided the three "Secrets of Fatima" to them. About half a million pilgrims come to celebrate this anniversary every year.

Knock, Ireland
A mysterious, silent, yellow-cloaked Mary appeared in the little village of Knock in 1879. Pilgrims began to arrive the following year and today they number in their thousands. The feast day of Our Lady of Knock is August 21.

Monserrat, Spain
More than a million pilgrims
visit the little Black Madonna,
La Moreneta, in the hills above
Barcelona every year.

Guadalupe, Mexico
Our Lady of Guadalupe is patroness
of the Americas and helped to bring
Christianity to the indigenous
people of the New World. About
12 million pilgrims come to her
huge modern shrine in Mexico
City every year.

20th-Century Apparitions

1968 Zeitoun, Egypt
Mohammad Atwa and about 200 other people saw a shining apparition of the Virgin above the Coptic Church. Later it was televised and seen by millions of Egyptians—Muslims and Christians alike.

1981 Medjugorje, Bosnia
The Virgin was seen by and spoke to six village teens. She brought a message of peace and reconciliation—just before bloody conflict tore the region apart.

1981 Kibeho, Rwanda
Again the Virgin appeared to six teenagers and brought news of coming conflict and bloodshed. She asked for a church to be built in Kibeho, dedicated to the Gathering of the Dispossessed.

1990s Marian apparitions were recorded in Cameroon, Ukraine, Iraq, Ireland, Australia, the United States, Peru, Italy, Canada, and Slovakia.

Mary's Feast Days

There are at least 40 days of the year when the Virgin is celebrated and that is not including local festivals. The entire month of May is also dedicated to her and occasionally, the Pope will declare a "Marian Year." Here are the six main feast days, several of which have pre-Christian origins.

February 2 Purification of the Blessed Virgin
Presentation of Jesus at the Temple.

March 25 The Annunciation
The Angel Gabriel tells Mary she will give birth to Jesus.

May 31 The Visitation
Mary visits her cousin Elizabeth.

August 15 The Assumption
She rises bodily to heaven.

September 8 Nativity of Our Lady
Her birthday.

December 8 The Immaculate Conception
The day she was conceived.

Text Credits

Every effort has been made to contact copyright holders; in the event of an inadvertent omission or error, please notify the editorial department at Ryland Peters & Small, Kirkman House, 12–14 Whitfield Street, London W1T 2RP.

Ryland Peters & Small wishes to thank the following writers, publishers, and literary representatives for the permission to use copyright material:

"Tribute to the Angels," by HD (Hilda Doolittle), from TRILOGY, copyright © 1945 by Oxford University Press; Copyright renewed 1973 by Norman Holmes Pearson. Reprinted by permission of New Directions Publishing Corp.

"Jesus, the Actor, Plays the Holy Ghost" by Anne Sexton. Reprinted by permission of PFD on behalf of Anne Sexton, © Anne Sexton.

Picture Credits

Jacket © Richard Jenkins 2003; 3 © Richard Jenkins 2003; 10 © Christina Dameyer/Lonely Planet Images; 14 © Vincent L. Long; 19 © Richard I'Anson/Lonely Planet Images; 22 Tom Leighton; 27 © Brian Leonard /runningfilm@optusnet.com.au; 31 © Jeffrey Becom/Lonely Planet Images; 34 © Chuck Jones; 39 © Doug Menuez/Getty Images; 40 © Greg Hadel/Hadel Productions; 45 ©Julie Nightingale/adamhouse.com; 50 Polly Wreford; 55 © Richard Jenkins 2003; 57 © Ray Laskowitz/Lonely Planet Images; 61 Andrew Wood.